MW01517859

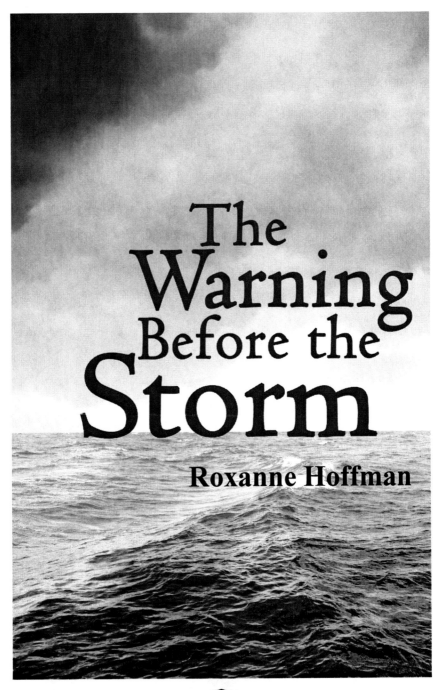

The
Warning
Before the
Storm

Roxanne Hoffman

authorHOUSE®

AuthorHouse™
1663 Liberty Drive
Bloomington, IN 47403
www.authorhouse.com
Phone: 1-800-839-8640

Published by AuthorHouse   11/14/2012

ISBN: 978-1-4389-0519-8 (sc)
ISBN: 978-1-4389-0520-4 (hc)

CONTENTS

ACKNOWLEDGEMENTS

TO MY LORD AND Savior. Words cannot express my love and gratefulness to you. Thank you for choosing me as the vessel that you spoke through to warn the people "Before The Storm". You are so worthy and may you always be highly exalted in my life. Thank you to the Author and Finisher of my faith. What an awesome God I serve, praise be to you forever more, my God and my king.

To my husband Timothy, I thank God that He gave me you. Thank you for not complaining about the endless nights that I stayed up writing and did not come to bed. I love you.

To my daughter Stephanie, thank you for being there for me and encouraging me to keep on writing, in the days of frustrations and discouragements. Our Lord used you to help hold my hands up. May He give you all the desires of your heart, I love you my precious daughter.

To my son-in-law Phil, thank you for the countless hours you sat at the computer typing over and over. I pray God will bless you abundantly.

To Pastor Denny and Shelley, thank you for the non-compromising word that you teach. You have impacted my life greatly and I love you both with all my heart.

To my son Eric who I love so much, thank you for your honesty and vision.

To Joni Liljedahl and the Abundant Life Church design team, thank you for an awesome cover. May God bless you abundantly for all your help.

INTRODUCTION

THERE WAS A MAN of God who came to me right before I was ready to move from Pennsylvania to Louisiana and he said, *"Roxanne, God wants you to write a book on the end times before his return"*. I sought the Lord as He started to speak into my spirit. He told me that so many people are being led astray and deceived. He said, "my people need to hear what the spirit is saying in these last days so they can prepare for the storm that is coming". He told me to warn the church while there is still time and to warn them means to caution one concerning his or her actions.

In the following pages that is exactly what our Lord is going to do. I am only being obedient to write about the things that our Lord desires for his church to know. Come, journey with me as the church sees and hears what the spirit is saying.

CHAPTER ONE

The Chilly Church

I CAN REMEMBER THE severe snowstorms we use to get when I lived in Pennsylvania. I can recall one dark, snowy night, as I looked out my window, how beautiful it was. The snow was laying on the trees and branches. It was like another world, one where everything was pure and clean. Then the Lord spoke to me and said, *"my child, this is how beautiful and clean anyone can be who has been washed by the blood of the lamb"*. It doesn't matter how dirty the sin or what it is, what matters is my word that says *though your sins are like scarlet, they shall be as white as snow* (Isaiah 1:18).

The bible describes our Lords appearance as lightning and his clothes white as snow. Revelation tells us that the *bride of Christ will be clothed in the linen* (Rev. 19:8). White represents purity and God is looking for people to love him and serve him with a pure heart. If we love our Father and *Lord with all of our heart and soul, mind, and strength* (Mark 12:30), then we will be able to love others the way He wants us to. We must remember that in our own flesh this is impossible, but as we surrender our lives to Him daily, He will take out that natural love in our hearts and replace it with His love.

This is the church that our Lord told *Peter that on this rock, I will build my church that the gates of hell will not prevail* (Matt 16:18).

Why church is the devil overcoming so many of God's people? Could it be that we pick and choose those ones that we want to love? Why don't we love the way He has commanded us to love? If they have a different skin color, are poor instead of rich, or a different nationality, we must all remember where we have come from and what our Lord has done for each of us. It doesn't matter what the sin was, for a sin is a sin and He died for each and every one of them.

Some of us have been pulled from the gutter of drugs and alcohol. Others he pulled from the wreckage of divorce, a broken family, a cesspool of pornography, adultery, witchcraft, and others He saved from false religion. Why is it that the church judges instead of loving? When the adulteress was brought before Jesus all those around him wanted to stone her but Jesus said to them, *if any is among us that has not sinned, then cast the first stone.* He knew that they all were sinners even though they could not recognize it.

For the word says, *we have all sinned and fell short of the glory of God* (Rom 3:23). He did not respond the way the crowed thought He should of. Instead He told her *go and sin no more.* It was the love coming from Jesus that touched this sinful woman's heart. His heart spoke forgiveness not judgment. Can you imagine how she felt?

For the first time in her life she was accepted and loved for who she was. We are not to condone the sin, but we are to love the sinner. Our reaction and response towards the sinner could determine their outcome. What would your reaction be if a prostitute, man with an earring or long hair, or person with facial piercings came walking down the isle of your church? What about the biracial couples and the woman who has children out of wedlock?

If we call ourselves a Christian, then the answer is simple. We would respond to these people the same way our Lord responded to the adulteress woman, out of love. How are we going to win the lost if we shun them? Let's remember the story of Zacchaeus and how the crowd complained when our Lord honored him with His fellowship. Zacchaeus was despised and hated by all of Israel.

He cheated the people, but Zacchaeus wanted to see Jesus, the Great Teacher, whom he heard was the Messiah, and Healer. Zacchaeus had climbed into a sycamore tree to catch a glimpse of Jesus as He was passing by. When Jesus saw Zacchaeus, He didn't look at him as a cheating tax collector, but as a servant who invited him into his home. Jesus honored Zacchaeus, and because of it, salvation came to his household (Luke 19:1-9). This is the love Jesus is talking about.

Ask yourself, how would you have responded? Would you have been cold and uncaring or would you have been full of compassion and love? Too many people want to be in a high position. They have a desire to be part of a committee, praise team, or teach to be recognized, but this is a lie from the enemy of our soul. Jesus tells us that, *he opposes the proud, but gives grace to the humble.* (John 4:6).

It's not about what position we hold with man, but how we serve the Lord. Jesus says that if you want *to be first, then you must be the very last and a servant of all* (Mark 9:35). If you want to be a lowly servant of the most High it means going unnoticed and unmentioned. These are the disciples that our Lord is looking for and calling out. When he chose the twelve disciples, he did not pick men who had money, fancy homes, a big car, or an important job, but He picked twelve nobody's.

They were unlearned and uneducated men who would turn this world upside down for Him. We must remember that it's not about positions in a church, but whether or not we serve and love as He did. Let us not forget that *our Lord did not come to be served, but to serve and gave His life as a ransom for many* (Matt 20:28). How many are willing to lay down their life for a brother? How many are willing to love as He loves?

How many are willing to leave everything behind to follow Him? How many are willing to serve Him, no matter what the cost? Let me answer that for you, not many! That's why He told us *many our called, but few are chosen* (Matt 22:14). It is time for the body of Christ to rise up and love as He has commanded us to love.

First we must love Him with all of our heart, soul, mind, and strength. Second we are to *love our neighbors as ourselves* (Matt 22:37-39). When we start loving each other despite a person's skin color, how much money he does or doesn't have, and whether he is educated or unlearned, we will then respond to sinners the way our Lord did, out of love. Remember you are to love the sinner, and not the sin. Then, and only then, will we see God move in our life.

We must do what our Lord has commanded us to do, love. When we seek God's will in our lives, and (His will is obedience to His word) die to self, there is nothing impossible for God. The church needs to stop being so cold and chilly, and start loving and forgiving. The reason the church is in this condition is because they are filled with to much self and not enough of His spirit, to much doing it man's way and not God's way, to much judging one another instead of loving one another, to much gossip and strife, instead of praying for one another and to much unforgiveness instead of forgiving those ones who has hurt and offended us. How can we say we love Jesus when we do nothing to help a fallen brother or sister?

How can we say we love Jesus when we do not help those in need or cannot love our own family? We need to stop looking at a person's outward appearance and let God show us the heart of that person. Their heart could be crying out for help, the same way each and every one of us cried out at one time. The church is in the condition it is in today because we have not obeyed His word. Don't you think it's time to start taking God at His word?

Let us not forget that love held Jesus to the cross at Calvary and His love is still their today for each and every one of us. As you surrender and allow the potter to remold and remake you, you will then no longer have a cold and chilly heart. It will be replaced with a heart full of His compassion, mercy, grace, forgiveness and love. Let us heed the warning in (Rev. 2:4), repent and return to our first love. There is no other way, because He tells us in his word that on *that Day, He will say away from me.*

I do not know you, workers of iniquity (Matt 7:22). So let's repent and do the works you did at first. Then you shall eat from the tree of life, which is in the midst of the paradise of God. What a promise that He has given each and every one of us. It is a promise to those of us who walk in obedience to his word. So don't you think it is time that we glow with our Father's love?

Let not only the lost see it, but finally feel it a heart full of His love, His heart, His love.

THE GIFT

"O" my Lord I need to know,

Why do You love me so?

As I look in the mirror at what I see,

I allow You to open my heart to the real me.

When I fall so short and I'm so full of pain,

I look ahead to the prize I will gain.

When I see the stripes upon Your back,

I fall on my knees when I realize how much I lack.

As I seek Your face each waking hour,

I pray to be filled with Your Holy power.

There are days that I feel that I'm losing my way,

That's when I have to remember the price that You paid.

As I'm swept away by the treacherous waves,

I'll never forget the life that You gave.

As I cry for help and call Your name,

I see the Cross and how You were shamed.

When I fight to hold on and can't take anymore,

That's when You allow me to see the crown of thorns that You wore.

So when I am swept away by all these floods,

I then lift my head and thank God for "Your Blood".

CHAPTER TWO

The Midway Church

MANY YEARS AGO I made my first trip to Israel, I remember climbing up a steep road, and at the top I saw the garden and the tomb. Halfway up the long stretch of road I did not think I was going to make it. Regardless of how I was feeling I kept striving until I had reached the top of the long road, which took us into the garden. As I walked through the garden of Gethsemane, I was in awe of how massive the Olive Trees were. They were as tall as they were wide. Later that day, I had learned that they were over two thousand years old.

While I climbed down the steps, which led toward the tomb, all I could do was cry thinking of what Jesus had done for me. I was so overwhelmed with thankfulness and love. To think if I had quit halfway up that hill, I would have missed out on this priceless experience. Then, why church is the body of Christ missing out? Why are there so many halfway Christians in the house today?

As I remembered that day, and what Jesus had done for me, I asked myself where would I be today if He only committed halfway to us? I thought about the garden. How Jesus was wrestling with His own flesh. His spirit was willing, but His flesh was weak. Knowing what was before Him, He cried out *Abba Father, everything is possible for you. Take this cup from me, but not my will but thy will* (Mark 14:36).

Jesus did not quit even though He knew what was ahead of Him. He pressed on to accomplish the will of the Father. Thank God He perservered, or we would be in total darkness and death, instead of light and life. Knowing church what our Lord has done for us, why do we compromise so easily? Why do we have one foot in serving God and the other foot in serving the world?

This cannot be, we cannot be half hearted Christians. We need to be whole—hearted believers and followers of Christ. It's time for the body of Christ to arise and go forth in the name of our Lord. It is time we quit condoning sin and compromising our beliefs in order to please man. Jesus was not concerned about offending those in sin or error.

Instead He pointed them out, tried to get them to repent, but their hearts refused His rebuke. It is time that the church stops living as the world just to please man. Jesus has called us to be different, we are not to talk as the world talks or do as the world does. We are not to party as the world nor are we to entangle ourselves with the sins of this world. Can you imagine how grieved our Father in heaven is when we fall into temptations?

We are supposed to be a witness and example of His son, but we fail because we refuse to say no. It is better to offend someone by saying no, then to grieve your heavenly Father by saying yes. There is nothing more disheartening than to witness to someone who says they want no part of being a Christian, because all so and so does is talk about their pastor and go to bars. This has happened to me, and because of the compromise in the churches, the world has a sour taste in their mouth for Christianity. I always tell people that Jesus loves them and you cannot judge a book by its cover.

Jesus delivered his people out of Egypt, so why are we always going back in? It is because we are not content with what He has given us, but we always want more. We get tired of waiting on the Lord so we chose to do things our own way. We want to be more like the Jones when we can't even tithe like He has commanded us to do. Admit it, we still want the ways of Egypt.

This cannot be anymore, for God said come ye out. A few years ago when I was recovering from my illness, I watched Lifetime movies everyday. Then one day the Lord spoke to me and said *my child what are you doing?* Lord I said I am watching true movies. He answered me and said, yes my child you are, movies concerning the violence in this world, movies about adultery, rape, and murder.

Even though I tried to justify my actions, I was unable to. I knew at that moment that I had been compromising the word of God. His word says we need *to put on the mind of Christ and to think on things lovely, pure, honest, true, and just, if anything is excellent or praise worthy—think about such things* (Phil 4:8). I thank God for His Holy Spirit, which convicts. I fell on my knees in repentance and from that day forward I stopped watching those types of movies.

We need to get rid of the junk in our lives so we can hear the Spirit of God as He is correcting and convicting us. Jesus warned the Nicolatians about the compromising that they were doing. We have allowed the pagan society that we are living in today to come into the church. It is being taught that spiritual liberty gives them the okay to practice idolatry and immorality. We have over looked this type of behavior for to long.

We are always trying to justify our sins and why we are compromising, but there is no justifying disobedience. God's word clearly states that *His wrath comes on the sons of disobedience* (Eph. 5:6). There are too many churches out there today doing it their own way, and seeking their own will. They try to get things done by operating in the flesh, while allowing man to have his own way in the house of God. These churches do not allow His spirit to correct or convict them, and because of it, they have over looked the sin that is in the churches today. Does not God tell us that *judgment begins in the house of God* (1 Peter 4:17).

It is time that the half-hearted Christians stop justifying their actions and sins. Sin is sin and there is no justifying it. Especially when we continue to do wrong, when we know what is right. We try to justify our actions even though we know they're wrong. For example, watching r-rated movies, going to bars, drinking, and allowing our children to participate in the pagan holiday of Halloween.

There is no justification when we allow abortion for any reason, saying it's the mother's choice. No church, it is murder! There is no justification when we allow homosexuals to stand in the pulpit and preach, for this is an abomination to God. There is no justification when you willingly choose to acknowledge and participate in the devil's activities of this world. When we have leaders who are compromising their beliefs and faith to please man, and allowing a man, proclaiming he is the Messiah to be on national television, we have a problem. If we stand by and watch, and say nothing, then we also are compromising the word of God.

When we know what is right and we choose to compromise by doing what's wrong, we then open ourselves up. Then, Satan, the enemy of our soul comes to attack and we suffer the consequences because of our disobedience. Our actions and our life will either represent Jesus or Satan. *We cannot serve two masters* (Matt. 6:24). We must remember what happened in the days of Noah. They were eating, drinking, marrying, and being given in marriage and all mankind was destroyed except for Noah's family (which was eight), because they refused to heed Noah's warning.

The church today is still refusing to heed the voice of the Lord, because of this, they to will be destroyed. If we continue to serve God half-hearted and continue to disobey His word so we can satisfy the cravings of the flesh, we to shall perish. Let us remember what Jesus has done for us. If you have been a half-hearted Christian and have compromised His word, ask Jesus to forgive you. Remember, He loved us so much, that He finished what He had started up on the tree at Calvary.

Isn't it time, that the church arises and *presses on towards the mark of the prize which is the high calling of God in Christ Jesus* (Phil 3:14)? Do not ever forget how much our Lord loves us. This is why He is warning us of the approaching storm. He does not want us to be swept away as man was in the days of Noah. However, He will not overstep man's free will. From this day forward, *choose whom you will serve, because you cannot waiver between two opinions. If the Lord is God, follow him* (1 Kings 18:21). *To him who overcomes, I will give some of the hidden manna. I will also give him a white stone with a new name written on it, known only to him who receives it* (Rev. 2:17).

SEA OF FORGIVENESS

As I watch the waves crashing in from the sea,
You speak to my spirit just trust in me.
As I swim in waters so deep and so clear,
You speak to my heart there's no need to fear.
As I swim in waters that's over my head,
pray to God for my flesh to be dead.
As I walk in the sand and fall on my knees,
I thank You Lord for setting me free.
As I cry out to You I want to go deep,
You opened my eyes and showed me a peep.
As you seek the Lord He shall be found,
Your chains will fall off and you'll no longer be bound.
As majestic is the beautiful sea,
You said my child, "My glory shall be".
As I long for Your glory to shine through me,
All men one day shall bow their knee.
The sand is so clean, so white, and so pure,
I know in my heart I have to endure.
As I sit at night looking at the dark sea,
I hear You say just hunger for me.
As I listen to the waves that are so loud and clear,
I thank You my God that You wipe every tear.
As I desire my God to just dive in,
I praise Your name for bearing my sin.
As the ocean and blue sky look like they meet,
My heart cries out to sit more at Your feet.

As wide and as deep is Your magnificent sea,
You tell me Lord that's how much You love me.
So every time I see the sea of blue,
I am reminded my Lord that Your love is true.
And as I sit and listen to the wind and waves,
I thank You Lord for Your blood that saves.

CHAPTER THREE

The Spoiled Church

WHEN I WAS A child, I use to love going to my grandmother's house. In the summer, she used to grow the most beautiful flowers. She had rows and rows upon rows of Zinnias and Gladiolus. My favorite flower was the Gladiolus. They grew to be tall and colorful. The array of colors reminded me of the rainbow. This type of plant required full sunlight and plenty of water.

It is a plant that produces flowers and seed from the same root structure year after year. There is nothing that can kill this plant unless it was dug up and its roots exposed. The Gladiolus would grow year after year. Its roots were so deep in the ground that it was able to draw water and nourishment from the soil. We as Christians must be rooted in Christ Jesus so we allow nothing to spoil our branches, and stop us from bearing fruit for Him.

If we allow the cares of this world, and unrepentant sin to suffocate and strip us from our lifeline, we will never produce the type of fruit our Lord is looking for. We have allowed *the small foxes to spoil the vineyard* (Sns 2:15). The Lord would ask, why are the foxes in my church spoiling my vineyard? Is it because a fox sets out to deceive its prey, and because of its slyness and craftiness?

We have allowed the Jezebels of this world to infiltrate our churches. We have accepted sexual immorality, this allowing it to be on the rampage.

Homosexuals are not only allowed to flaunt their sin in public, but also to stand behind the pulpit and preach that this type of life style is acceptable in today's society. No church it is not, God warns us *that no homosexual or immoral person will inherit the kingdom of God* (1 Cor.6:9). Why as believers are we intimidated by this type of sin?

Could it be that part of our heart has accepted this behavior, instead of rejecting it, and standing up for the truth? We have tolerated and allowed teachers and pastors to teach a gospel, that this type of lifestyle and behavior is ok. The Lord would ask His churches today, *you were running a good race, who has hindered you from the truth?* (Gal. 5:7). We have allowed man to bring in his ideas and his ways. They have corrupted the word of God to fit their society in which they are living in today.

This type of gospel teaches that if you are struggling financially and if you are being afflicted that you must have sin in your life. It is a gospel from the pits of hell, because God's word tells us that we will suffer as Christ suffered and we will have *trials and tribulations in this world,* but Jesus says, *I have overcome the world* (John 16:33). Any true follower of our Lord who is on the straight and narrow path will always have afflictions. God has promised us that *He would deliver us from all of them* (psalm 34:19).

It is time for the church of Christ to arise and stand up for the truth. We must call sin for what it is, and stand up for the truth, no matter what the cost. If we don't walk out this truth we will never come to pass. The church of Christ must stop tolerating the coarse joking and perverseness that is among us in the house today.

We need to stop being a spoiled Christian and start becoming a fruit bearer. We must nurture our spirit man daily by being in fellowship with Him, feeding on His word, and drinking from the Living Water. This is where we allow the cleansing power of His Holy Spirit, to help rid us of the foxes that are trying to kill God's vineyard. When we allow God's truth to cultivate the area around our heart, then and only then, will we produce fruit that is pleasing to our Father.

When we allow His spirit to help rid us of all bitterness, pride, unforegiveness, anger, jealousy, selfishness, gossip, worry, complaining, fear, doubt, idolatry, and any immoral thoughts or behavior, then His spirit can flow through us and help us to be fruit bearers. The Holy Spirit can only flow through a clean vessel. It is like the oil in the car. If we don't change it regularly then it becomes thick and dirty and begins to clog, slowing down the flow of oil going to the engine.

This is what happens in a believer's life when we do not allow God's spirit to clean us. When there is unrepentant sin that does not get confessed, it eventually will stop the flow of the Holy Spirit, because He cannot flow through a clogged or dirty vessel. We serve a Holy God and His spirit can only flow through holy vessels. *He has called us to be holy, because He is holy* (1 Peter 1:16) and without *holiness no one can see God* (Heb. 12:14).

We must always allow God's word, which is truth, to settle in and become productive. This can only happen to a person who has a humble and pure heart after the things of God who puts God first, and loves him with all their heart, soul, mind, and strength. Someone who tells God, not my way, but your way, not my word, but your word, not my will but your will, and is willing to give up their desires to have a heart that totally follows Him.

We must always be clothed in humility and have the mind of Christ. We need to stop doing it our way, and allow the Holy Spirit to cleanse and convict us. When we are willing to die to the flesh daily, then our lives will produce the fruit that our Lord wants. We must remember that the fertilizer we use determines the fruit we produce in our personal lives.

If we feed on the word of God daily, and allow the Spirit to prune the areas that are infested with the small foxes, we then will bear fruit for the kingdom of God. If we feed on the world and its ways, and do not allow the Spirit to get rid of all the infestation of sin and self, then we will produce fruit of the flesh, which will please the father of lies, Satan himself. The church today is on a *sick bed of afflictions because prolonged unconfessed sin will bring great tribulation into a believer's life* (Rev. 2:21-23).

It is time to heed the warning and stand up for *truth or you to shall perish* (2 Thess. 2:10). Remember that Jesus has called us to *bear fruit, fruit abundantly* (John 15:16). He loved us so much that He took our fall, so lets become and bear that which He is worthy of. Lets hold on to His promise that he who overcomes, I will give power over the nations and you shall receive the Morning Star. Let us remember that what we are is His gift to us, but what we become, is our gift to Him.

THE BLESSING IN THE THORN

Oh, my Lord you know all about pain,

He says to me, press on for the prize you will gain.

The days are short and the nights are long,

Trust in Me, and I'll make you strong.

Cry out to You and give You the praise,

The day is coming and You will be raised.

As I lift my eyes to Your heavenly hills,

You speak to me, my child just be still.

I pray my Lord please take this thorn,

Then He says to me, look at the crown I wore.

I pray my Lord; I need more grace,

His reply to me is just finish your race.

As I lay there seeking your Holy face,

Your loving arms, they always embrace.

As I lay in my bed so full of pain,

You sing to me, again and again.

As I tell you my Lord I love You so,

You remind me always You'll never let go.

As I cry to my Lord, I can't take no more,

He speaks to my spirit, one day you will soar.

As I just surrender for His will to be done,

I thank you Lord, You're my Holy one.

As I strive to persevere each waking day,

One day my Lord, my crowns I will lay.

Then He said my child I'm molding you,

And whispers in my ear, your one of the few.

CHAPTER FOUR

The Lifeless Church

WHEN I THINK OF something being dead, it means to be lifeless. This was how my life was before I met Jesus. I was a good person and I went to church, yet my life had no meaning. I was married to a wonderful man and I had three beautiful children, yet I always felt empty. Though I was walking around very much alive, I was dead (spiritually). I was always searching for happiness and looking for acceptance from others, never finding it.

Then one day a storm came blowing my way, with my marriage in jeopardy, and I had no where to turn. After confronting my husband with the truth, he knew that he was caught and he started to confess everything to me, I wanted to die. In one of the darkest moments of my life, this man of God came to my business I owned and started to tell me that I needed Jesus. I told him to get out and cursed at him.

Then my husband came to me and told me he was leaving me, he did not love me anymore and did not know if he wanted the other woman or not. Needless to say, I hit rock bottom. I tried to take my own life, but God in His mercy spared me. I went to work afterwards, and here comes this man of God once again. He asked me, are you ready yet? At that moment in my life, I was so desperate that I said yes. That is when he told me about Jesus. From that moment on, I fell in love with Him and that was the happiest day of my life.

You see church; He turned my unhappiness into joy, my disappointments into hope, and my confusion into peace. Though my marriage was dead, I stood on His word that *what God has put together let no man separate* (Mark 10:9). I vowed that I would love him for better or worse and that I was going to ride out this storm. It wasn't easy and so many times I wanted to leave, but I knew I couldn't. If I had left my husband, I would have been out of the will of God for my life.

I feared too much to be out from under His protection. Though the years passed and my husband was doing everything to earn back the trust and love that was lost, nothing seemed to be working. It was no longer he, but it was I. I couldn't let go of the betrayal and hurt that he had caused my children and I. I knew then that I was no longer in love with this man. Not knowing what to do, I did the only thing that I knew how, pray.

I stood on God's promises, while I was asking Him to help me let go and teach me how to forgive. I pleaded with the Lord to let me fall in love with my husband again. Then it suddenly happened, I watched our Lord resurrect my marriage back to life once again. I stood in awe as he took this lifeless marriage and restored it into a new life with new beginnings.

Only our Lord can bring back to life, that which was dead. I am more in love with my husband today then I was over thirty years ago. I have watched my prayer come to pass where all I wanted was for my husband to love me as Christ does. I often reflect back on my life and wonder what would have happened, if I had left Tim. I knew that I had to persevere because my marriage was worth it.

There are so many believers out there who are walking around spiritually dead. They think that they are alive, but they are dead. They have allowed the offenses from others to cut off their main lifeline, which is Jesus Christ. You see church, our trials and afflictions can either make us bitter or better, the choice is ours. The church today *has a form of Godliness, but denies its power* (2Tim 3:5).

The Lord would ask His church today, what has caused you to be weak and for you to fall asleep? Could it be the evil eye of power that has crept in among us? The Word warns us that certain men and woman have crept in unnoticed. These ungodly people appear to be alive, so they can deceive the weak and turn the grace of God into lascivious.

Is it possible that these people go to church, serve on committees, shake our hands, and even preach the word of God, when all along they are spots in your love feasts? (Jude 12). These so called believers have crept in to weaken those who are strong in Jesus with their many persuasive words. They are everyday people who are quick to judge you, but yet say God bless you. They are the Judas' of this world with only one motive in mind, to betray those ones closest to him.

They are the faith speakers until the storm hits. We must remember that Judas deceived everyone around him, because he had the evil eye of power. He appeared very much alive, though he was very much spiritually dead. These believers seek the thrill of His power, yet they do not know the One who saved them. They call Him Lord only to receive from Him.

While in the mean time, they don't even know Him or give Him the time of day. They believe that they are holier and spiritually above others. They quote a few scriptures so others believe that they know His word, but even the demons know the word of God. They know nothing about Jesus and try to fool all of those around them, but they cannot fool God.

These are those ones who satisfy the cravings of their flesh; yet know nothing about walking in the Spirit of God. They believe that they're doing good works when all along their works are dead. Jesus makes it quite clear in His word that only those who know Him, and have done the will of the Father, will inherit eternal life. Many, and I say many, on that day will say *Lord, Lord, but Jesus' reply will be, I do not know you, you workers of iniquity* (Luke 13:25-27).

Let us not forget Cain and how he thought he was more righteous than his brother. Because of this, he killed him. Could it be, he had the evil eye of power? Let us remember that wherever the evil eye of power goes, it kills the good and leaves destruction. Jesus warned us in His word *to take heed that no one would deceive you* (Eph. 5:6).

It is time for the church to stop seeking the power and seek His face and will. He tells us that we need to *strengthen what remains or it will die* (Rev. 3:2). *The Holy Spirit will not always strive with man* (Gen. 6:3). The angels that left their first estate were destroyed because of an evil eye of power (Jude 1:6). Notice that these angles were created perfect. So, is it possible that this same evil eye of power is roaming around in the churches today?

Let's not forget what happened when strife came into Abraham and Lot's camp. God allowed it to see what choice man would make. Abraham humbled himself and let Lot chose first which way he would go. Abraham told him "I will go the opposite way of you." The evil eye of power caused Lot to chose the green and fertile land, which he thought was the best, because it looked good only to find out later that he had made the wrong choice.

When the motives of our heart are wrong, we are bound to make wrong decisions. It is time for the body of Christ to mind their own business and to be about the Father's business. It is time for the church to operate in the power of His Holy Spirit and not in the flesh. As the church begins to humble themselves, *then God says, that He will exalt us in due season* (1Peter 5:6).

Heed the warning church. Do not seek power, but strengthen that which is about to die and remain humble. Then His power will find you. It is only in His holy presence that we realize we can do nothing and are nothing without Him. It is time to wake up before it's too late. After all, the thief will come at an hour you do not know.

Let us not forget how much Jesus loves each and every one of us. So let the church repent and ask the Lord to help us not to murmur, complain, or to walk in our own lusts, speaking swelling words to please man. Also, not to take advantage of the poor and weak, but be ready to help no matter what the need is, whether physical or spiritual. Help us to have the fear of God in our lives once again and let all man live to see His kingdom come.

To him who overcomes they shall be clothed in white garments and I will not blot out his name from the Book of Life, but I will confess his name before my Father and before His angles (Rev. 3:5).

THE BROKEN VESSEL

My Lord, my Lord, I love You so,
My flesh is fighting; it won't let go.
Life's full of sorrow, disappointment, and pain,
I must press on for the prize I will gain.
I want to soar; I want to fly,
Then you spoke to my heart, it is time to die.
As I lay in my bed the thoughts fill my head,
As Your Spirit tells me your flesh must be dead.
Though my heart and my Spirit are so full of tears,
I'm thankful my Lord for the cross that You bared.
So many questions, so many whys,
My tears fill Your bottle each time that I cry.
Though the mountains are tall and the valleys are low,
You're there when I call, promising never to let go.
Through the valleys I walk, through the valleys I go,
I'll never forget how You love me so.
When I chose to let go of all of me,
Then my Master will say, come and you shall see.
As I stand in Your presence and bow my knee,
All earthly desires they have to flee.
As the eagle soars from up on high,
I have to press on; I have to fly.
As I hear His voice and seek His face,
I'll never forget it's all because of grace.
So when I feel crushed and oh so down,
One day very soon, I'll be given a crown.

CHAPTER FIVE

The Lacking Church

I WAS A MEMBER of a church of about three hundred people for almost ten years in Pennsylvania. After God had completely healed me, He spoke to my husband and myself to move on to another church. We had met a pastor of a small church at a meeting, and we fell in love with the man of God. We were only in that church for about four months when God moved us down south.

I was found myself at a spirit filled church where they knew about God's love. They not only knew about it, but they showed His agape love towards everyone that came through the doors. I had never felt so accepted in my life, as I did in this church. The man and woman of God preached such truth, that I couldn't wait to go back every week. I can remember telling my pastor, that I knew God was going to put us back into a small church.

His reply to me was, Roxanne don't limit God. I can recall the last service we went to on Sunday before we moved. I told God that I had finally found a church that I can call home, and now He is moving me on. I was set free to worship Him in this church; after all, I am a worshipper who loves to dance before the Lord. After going back and forth with God, I went to the altar just weeping before Him.

Then He spoke to me and said, "Roxanne, this church isn't even the icing on the cupcake for what I have planned for you and the church I have waiting for you". When the service was over we did not say good bye, but we told our pastor and his wife that we would see them later. When you tell someone goodbye, it is final, but we knew when we went home to visit, we would go back to that small church in the country.

We would go to encourage the man and woman of God who had impacted my life and my husband's life tremendously. Then, the day came when we moved to Louisiana and had to find a new church. After missing two weeks of church because we were busy settling in and learning the area, I was thirsty and hungry for God's word. We drove around looking for churches, but they were all so big.

I still felt in my spirit that we were going to be placed in a small church. One day at the pool, this woman told me about this church. I couldn't wait to go, but boy did I get a surprise. The church was huge and held around nine thousand people; the praise team looked like some type of orchestra. I never felt such a lack of warmth and love in a church before. There was no enthusiasm in the house of God at all.

Though the church appeared to have it all, they had nothing (spiritually). It was like one big theater where every one was getting ready to perform. I got up to leave, but God told me "no, stay where you are at". He said, "I have something to show you". As I sat there, I said to myself, where is God at in this place?

Where is His spirit? I was so grieved in my spirit at what I was seeing and hearing. Can you imagine how grieved our Heavenly Father was? Though they called Him Lord, and they appeared to be rich, they were spiritually dead. The church seemed to lack nothing, but they were lacking everything, His spirit. I left the service heavy and disappointed.

I kept asking God where He wanted us to go, but He kept silent. Then my husband and I went to another church the following Sunday, it was worse than the first. I did not want to go, because I knew in my spirit that this church also thought they had it all, but they are spiritually dead. My husband insisted, so we went, big mistake. If I would have been a newborn babe in the Lord and went to a church like this, I would have never wanted any part of Jesus.

These churches think they have it all, but they are so deceived. After leaving that service, I fell into a depression. My heart and spirit longed to be in fellowship with like—minded people. People who loved Jesus and whom His spirit led. I can remember calling my pastor back in Pennsylvania on a Monday. I asked him if God had spoken to him on where we should go to church.

His reply to me was "Roxanne, God said, you know that I am not to tell you". I would not leave the house because I was so low. Then it happened, God used a friend of mine from Pennsylvania, who loves Jesus as much as I do. She called me and said, "God told me to tell you to get out of you pity party". Look in the phone book under churches, and call them, and ask what they believe in.

I spent all day Tuesday calling churches; none of them seemed to arouse my spirit. The next day as I was driving to Wal-Mart, on a road that I had traveled about ten times already. The Lord spoke to me, "You see that building, pull in there on your way back". I had no idea that it was a church building. On the way home from Wal-Mart, I pulled into the parking lot and saw the sign with the name of the church, "Celebration of Hope".

God spoke once again to me and said, "You will be here at seven for tonight's service". I called my husband and told him God sent me to our church. We went that night and I knew immediately that I was home. I couldn't believe all the times that I had driven past this building and never realized it was a church.

I was finally in a church where the pastor and his wife love as Jesus loves. Yes church, God sent me to a small church. Though small in numbers, we are mighty in His spirit. I have never been to a church that is so one in Christ. You see church, it isn't the building that makes you a Christian it is the love of Christ in each of us.

It isn't about how many pews are filled with people, but it is about souls hearing the uncomprimised truth of the Word of God. It's not about the clothes we wear or the committees we serve on, but what matters is whom we serve (Christ or Satan). Many churches today think that because they are rich, they lack nothing. Jesus warns them and tells them that, *they need to anoint their eyes and put on the eye salve so they can see* (Rev. 3:20).

The church needs to be a servant for the Lord, and have His agape love for all mankind. This is the church that will overcome any obstacle that is before them. Their trust will be totally in their God, for He makes all things possible. It is time that the church stops huddling among themselves, for there are too many clicks in the body of Christ today. The Lord would ask, if we are suppose to be one in Him, why the favoritism? Let us not *forget that God has no favorites* (James 2:1).

It is not about how close we can become with the pastor or those in authority, but how close we become with Him. Let's not forget, it is suppose to be all about Jesus.

We must remember that *God is the potter and we are the clay and the work of His hand* (Isaiah 65:7). We must remember that Jesus left His high position in heaven to come to earth to serve.

Let's recall the time our *Lord washed the disciples feet to show us the example of servant hood* (John 13:13-5). Jesus even washed the feet of the one who He knew was going to betray Him. It is time that we who call ourselves Christians, stop looking at the outward appearance and start looking at the inward as Jesus does. It is time for the watchmen to sound the alarm and warn the people to repent and prepare themselves for the approaching storm. It is time *to work out our salvation with fear and trembling* (Phil 2:12).

We need to be soldiers who will stand up for righteousness sake. Soldiers who will march into the battlegrounds and reclaim this lost and dying world for Him. We need to let our light shine among the darkness, and be moved with compassion as He was. To show mercy as He shows us mercy, to forgive others as He has forgiven us, to serve Him as He came to serve, and to love as He loves us. *Let us not forget that there is none righteous, no not one* (Rom 3:10).

His word says that *if a righteous man turns from his righteousness and commits iniquity and does all the abominations that the wicked man does, shall he live? All the righteousness that he has done will not be remembered and he shall die* (Ezekiel 18:24). The church needs to realize that Jesus is our righteousness. If we are not in Him, we are unrighteous, and will die spiritually. Don't get swept away with the ways of this world, for Jesus tells us *we are not of the world, but we are in it* (John 8:23).

The churches today are so heavenly minded that they have become no earthly good. Jesus warns us that it is better to be hot or cold then lukewarm. Jesus said He would vomit the lukewarm out of His mouth. Jesus would say to the churches today, you say you are rich, have become wealthy and have need of nothing, but hear the word of the Lord, and take warning.

Jesus rejects the halfhearted efforts of self satisfied Christians. He describes these churches as *wretched, miserable, poor, blind, and naked* (Rev 3:17). He is warning all the churches through out the land that are spiritually self-deluded. These churches think they are wealthy and in need of nothing, because they are well clothed in expensive garments. When actually, they are spiritually impoverished and naked.

They also believe that their physical eyesight enables them to see spiritually, when they are actually blinded to spiritual realities. The Lord would say, "I love you, but you need to repent and become excited once again for the things of God. Let this lost and dying world see the zeal of the Father consume His house once again. To the over comer, you will share my throne saith the Lord".

THE GRATEFUL SERVANT

Oh my sweet Lamb of God,
Who sits upon the throne on high.
I long to hear Your voice each day,
Please help me walk in all Your ways.
As I seek Your Holy face,
I need Your strength to run this race.
Oh Lord, my heart's desire,
Is to be cleansed with Your Holy fire.
As I hunger for your holiness,
Let my life display Your grace.
I long to worship You always,
Let my light be full of rays.
I love You more and more each day,
My heart tells You, I won't go astray.
As I learn to wait on You,
My love for you will always be true.
As I bless Your holy name,
Change me Lord, to never be the same.
As I pray to You alone,
Help me to remember, You spoke to dry bones.
When I come to You my Father,
Let me drink from Your deep waters.
When my life is done on earth,
I'll live with You; I've been rebirth!

Chapter Six

The Persistent and Loyal Church

WHEN I THINK ABOUT being faithful, I recall the day I married my husband. He was my high school sweetheart and we married straight out of school. I vowed to love him and honor him in sickness and health, for richer or poorer, forsaking all others until death do us part. Little did I know at the time, the true meaning of those words?

At the age of eighteen, we thought we had it all together and we could conquer what ever came our way, boy were we wrong. They say that the first year of marriage is the hardest, but what about all of the years that follow? It was just the beginning of much suffering and sorrow in our lives. As we were blessed with three beautiful children, it required more of our loyalty to them then to each other.

As our kids were growing up, my marriage was growing apart. Circumstances and hardships happened that caused that faithfulness to be broken. When I found out that my husband had been unfaithful to me, I wanted to die. I had never felt so betrayed in my life. Little did I know that God had allowed this affliction to draw me to Him.

God does not tempt us to sin, but He knows what it will take to get our attention, and that definitely got mine. That's when I found Jesus. During the years of putting my marriage back together, I remained faithful to my husband. I wanted to leave him so many times, but I feared God too much. Besides, I had made a vow to love him until death.

I allowed God to do what needed to be done and because of it He restored my marriage. Imagine how God feels when we are unfaithful to Him. He desires our faithfulness. Let's not forget that without faith it is impossible to please God. I thank God that *He is faithful even when I am faithless* (2Tim 2:13).

To be faithful means, to be loyal to someone. How do we think God feels when we are not faithful to Him, when He has called us to step out in faith? We allow our fears and doubts to overcome us, which prevents us from doing that very thing that He has called us to do. Think about the blessing that we are missing out on every time we don't walk in faith and how much it must hurt our Father, because I know how hurt I was do to my husband's unfaithfulness.

Jesus asked in His word, that when *He returns, would He find faith* (Luke 18:8)? To be the faithful church that's going to overcome in these last days, we must let go of our will to do the will of our Father. It is going where we can't see what is ahead of us. It is stepping out in faith not knowing what is going to happen. It's letting go of our dreams, hopes, plans, ways, and thoughts to be obedient in what He has called us to do, no matter what it may look like.

When all things seem impossible, know that *all things are possible in God* (Mark 10:27). When I was rushed to the hospital at the age of forty-three in kidneys and liver failure, I totally trusted in God. When the doctors said, "she is going to die, we don't think she will make it through the night", it was my faith that kept me alive. I believed that what God had promised, had not yet come to pass.

I believed my Lord when He spoke to me, "I am going to prove myself to my faithful servant". Although, at that time man said, "She will be going home on dialysis". Church He did exactly what He told me He was going to do. After a week on dialysis and plasma treatments, He supernaturally healed my kidneys and liver.

They began to function on their own once again. This is the type of faith our Lord is looking for. I'm no one special, just a sinner whose been saved by grace through faith.

I am just a willing vessel longing to be used to bring glory to our Lord through my many trials and tribulations. It's all about Jesus, and I know because I was always faithful in serving Him, He honored my faithfulness. God is calling His church to *walk by faith and not by sight* (2Cor 5:7). He is always testing us to see if we are going to be faithful. My illness, which lasted over three years, was a piece of cake compared to my next testing.

My husband was offered a job promotion requiring us to move out of state, I said, "no way"! I wrestled with God and told Him I was not leaving my children, grandchildren, family, and business behind. There was no way I was going to leave Pennsylvania and move to Louisiana. I carried on so much that God closed the door, which He had opened, but only for a season.

Though my flesh was happy, I felt uncomfortable in my spirit. I never quit praying not my will, but thy will be done. During those five months of the door being closed, God was dealing with my heart. One day the Lord said to me, "Roxanne, did you not tell me you would go where ever I would take you? Then why are you holding on to the things of this world? Your family, children, and business that I have given you, do not belong to you, but they belong to me".

Anyone who puts his or her hand to the plow and looks back is not worthy to follow Me (Luke 9:62). When I heard my Lord say those words to me, all I could do was fall on my knees and ask Him to forgive me, for my pride and my selfishness. One month later, we moved down south to Louisiana, leaving my comfort zone and all my loved ones behind. You see church, I knew in my heart and my spirit that God had called my husband and me down south.

Even though we had much opposition from family and Christian friends, we knew we had to be faithful to the one who has been faithful to us. There were many days of loneliness, fear, and doubts, but He has proven Himself to us over and over. He has filled the void in my heart with more of Him. God is looking for His churches to remain loyal no matter what the cost.

To pray when they don't feel like praying, give when they can't give no more, forgive when their flesh is telling them not to forgive, and love no matter what. We must remember that faith says, He is our Provider when we have no money, our Healer when we are sick, our Comforter in times of loss, our Peace in times of confusion, our Advocate when we are falsely accused, and our Joy in times of disappointment. He is the one who carries us when we can't carry on, our Hope when all hope is gone, our Light in the darkness, and He is the way, the truth, and the life when we are lost.

The faithful church knows who their God is and stands firm on the Solid Rock. He is their all and all no matter what the approaching storm looks like.

Remember, we serve a faithful God and He would say to His churches, "keep the faith and be strong in me. I am coming back for a church without spots or blemishes, and with me are my rewards for those who have kept the faith and have overcome.

My promise to those who have remained loyal to Me is the crown of life, and a place in God's presence with a new name and the New Jerusalem. Remember church, I am coming back for my bride that where I am she will be also".

SAFE HAVEN

I have a place where I can go, to my secret place for no one will know.

At this place I am not afraid to enter in, the price has been paid.

As I go to sit or bow my knee my heart cries out for my Lord to see.

As I sit and wait to hear His voice, He says "my child,
what is your choice?"

This ungodly world has nothing to offer; if you choose this
road you will not live.

I cry for the people who will go down this path for in the end,
they will all feel God's wrath.

On this path there is nowhere to hide,

Repent and choose the narrow road.

The path that is wide is full of sorrow and pain.

When you stay on this path, there will be no gain.

Why are people going down the wrong way?

Because they won't obey what the Word has to say.

Return to the narrow way before it's too late.

If you choose the wrong path, you'll seal your fate.

If you choose this path and continue down this road,

Remember to let go of your heavy load.

Not many people go down this path if you choose to follow you won't feel God's wrath.

Though difficult the way and few won't find.

If you stay on this path you'll have peace of mind.

You must have faith to get through the gate.

Without any faith it will be too late.

While on this path your will dies more and more.

Just keep your focus and every day you will soar.

As you strive each day to follow His way.

He will walk with you in the cool of the day.

When I cry to my Lord, this road is too hard.

I want you to remember how my face was marred.

As the Lord speaks to me, there's no other way.

By faith I must walk each and every day.

I have made my choice every time I pray.

With the Lord's help I won't ever stray.

So with a loud voice I will proclaim.

One day soon I will have a new name.

CHAPTER SEVEN

The Approaching Storm

I CAN REMEMBER THE first time I saw the ocean. My husband and I went on vacation to Florida with his cousin and wife. I stood there looking at the vastness of the ocean and it terrified me. As I started to swim out, a large wave swept over me and took me under. I ended up back on the shore thinking that this was enough for me.

I did not go back in because I was so afraid. Then when I met Jesus and fell in love with Him, I was drawn to the ocean like a magnet. My husband took me on a cruise to the Caribbean for our seventeenth anniversary. I can remember seeing the crystal clear blue waters and I stood in awe.

That's when I started to swim out deep. All fear had left me and my spirit man was swimming out, because *deep calleth to deep* (Psalm 42:7). My husband would stand on the shore yelling at me to come in. I fell in love with the ocean. I loved the sound of the rushing waves as they came onto the shore, and the peace and tranquility I felt as I walked the white sandy beaches.

As I grew in the Lord so did my longing to go back to the Caribbean. For our twenty-fifth anniversary my husband took me back. While we were sailing out of Puerto Rico, I wanted to bust a seam because I was so happy. I recall one day as I was looking out over the sea, the waters were dark, rough, and getting higher. I knew in my spirit that the Lord wanted to show me something. Then He spoke, "my child, this is what is coming. You will tell my people to get ready for the approaching storm".

I looked at my sister and told her that there's a storm coming that's going to take God's children by surprise and take them under. Only those who are anchored in Jesus Christ will not be swept away. I was vexed in my spirit for the rest of the cruise. When we docked in Puerto Rico my husband and I walked the beach for the last time.

As my husband was walking ahead of me, my Lord spoke once again. He said, "My child, I have something to show you". As I walked holding Jesus' hand I saw two sets of footprints in the sand. Then He said, "Watch this". The waves came onto the shore, and the water washed one set of footprints away. He said to me, "Remember when you think you can't go on, I will be carrying you".

Five months later I was in kidney and liver failure. God gave me a set of new kidneys and a new liver one-week later. He healed me by His supernatural power, but my body was affected greatly due to the physical shock on it. I spent nine months in bed from the after effects. I was always so weak that every time I stood up, I passed out. I had to be carried everywhere because I was too weak to walk on my own.

My body rejected all foods and I was unable to keep anything down or in. I ended up in the hospital every two to three weeks due to a lack of potassium. At times I would spend up to two weeks out of every month in the hospital. This affliction went on for two and a half years. There were many times I wanted to give up because I was so sick. Yet, in those times there was a flame of faith in me that kept holding on to God's promises.

I knew if God was able to supernaturally give me new kidneys and a new liver; He was able to heal my battered body. As I continued to go from doctor to doctor to find answers for this affliction, it came to the point that I could bear it no more. The pain was so severe that even the morphine didn't help. I didn't understand why, and at this point I asked my husband why God didn't take me home when I first went into kidney failure. My physical body could take no more and I was becoming spiritually weak.

Unable to do anything on my own, I just wanted to die already. I felt so inadequate, because I was unable to be a wife to the man I loved, nor a mother to my children. I was a grandmother who longed to hold her two newborn grandsons in her arms. Yet, in those darkest moments of my life Jesus manifested Himself to me. It was during the long hours of night that I recalled the vision on the beach.

It was all the times of being flat on my back that He revealed His love for me. In the times that I had such physical pain, and all I wanted to do was die, it was then that I realized how much our Lord had suffered for us. It was all the questions and not understanding why, that He was teaching me to trust Him more. He was teaching me to love and to have compassion on all mankind.

It was through all the years that I had to be given potassium, as it burned like a hot iron while it flowed through my veins that God was burning up all those things in my heart that needed to come out. I bear the scar today on my left hand from the burn that occurred from one of the times I had to be given potassium. As I look back over this trial and affliction, I thank God for everything that He allowed me to go through, because it has made me who I am today. I am so glad that His word was in my heart, that I was able to use it against the Devil and to remind God of His promises to me.

For all the times I was unable to be in church or to read the Bible, I am grateful that His word abided in me and carried me through this affliction. After three long years of suffering, it suddenly happened and God healed me completely. I learned through this affliction that *God's grace is sufficient for thee (2 Cor. 12:9).*

No matter what we have to endure or what storm we may have to face in our lifetime God's grace is sufficient. As I look back through the years, it is like it never happened to me, but I bear the scar on my hand. My Lord gave me the miracle of my life totally being restored. The Lord would say to His Church, "Prepare yourselves for the approaching storm".

We don't know when or how, but we know in the Spirit that it is coming. As I was in the wave pool on my last vacation, I swam into the deep waters so when the waves were released I could ride them out. I was in seven feet of water, when the Lord spoke to me once again. He said "My child, watch what I have to show you". The bell rang as a sign for the waves to begin, everyone in the pool started to scream and panic and run to the shallow waters.

As the six to eight foot waves swept over me, the force was so powerful that it took me under, but I came right back up. I watched all the people who were going under the water, being tossed to and fro, as they were being swept away by the waves. Then the Lord spoke again and said, "If man-made waves can take you under in a blink of an eye and cause such fear and panic, just think what my waves of wrath and judgment will do too those ones who do not know me and are disobedient to my word".

God wants His people to prepare for the storms that are approaching. If you are not built on the Solid Rock, which is Jesus, then you too will be taken under and washed away like the sand on the seashore. Don't run from the storm of life, but embrace them because God said in His word *that in all things He is works good for those who love Him* (Rom.

8:28). He wants us to give thanks in all things and to be able to say *it is good that I have been afflicted that I might learn thy statues* (Psalm 119:71).

We need to not be afraid because of the treacherous waters or the size of the waves, but to fear the creator who made the ocean and its waves. We need to *fear the one who is able to destroy both soul and body in Hell* (Matt. 10:28). We must remember that during these storms, He has promised us that the *waters shall not overflow thee* (Isaiah 43:2) nor *will He ever leave us nor forsake us* (Duet. 31:8). He wants His Church to make the necessary preparations for the approaching storms.

We need to know the word of God and stand in faith no matter how dark it gets or how high the waves are. We need to totally trust that *He is our very present help in time of trouble* (Psalm 9:9) no matter how hard the winds may blow. He wants us to rest in Him that during these storms we can speak *peace be still* (Mark 4:39). God doesn't want His vessels to be damaged from the crashing of the waves, but He wants us to stand on His word that the anchor holds.

Jesus wants us to be able to go in and pull those ones out of the treacherous waters and tell them about Him and His love for them. Jesus would say to His Church, "this is what it is all about". We need to get ready for the coming harvest. Jesus needs His servants to go into the fields and help bring those ones out who have been traumatized by the storms.

We must be willing to deny ourselves and pick up our cross daily to follow Him. We must be willing to lay down our life if that is what it takes to help someone in need. Let us not forget that our Lord laid down His life to help each and every one of us. So now *because He lives we will live also* (John 14:19). So let us be prepared to not be surprised for the day of the Lord shall come as a thief in the night!

Roxanne Hoffman

THE PERFECT STORM

Oh, my Lord I feel so heavy and blue,
I hear Your voice as I cry out to You.
The constant beating of the furious waves,
I reach for Your hands; they will always save.
As the raging waves crash over me,
I seek Your face so I can see.
As I take a beating every waking day,
My hearts desires to walk in Your Holy ways.
As I fight the waves to stay afloat,
Help me remember You're not in the boat.
As I try to swim in waters to deep,
I know one day a harvest I will reap.
As I fight for my life so afraid I will drown,
You say my child I'll give you a crown.
As I cry out to You I'm so tired and worn,
I then remember how Your body was torn.
I become weak as the waves go over my head,
To stay alive my flesh must be dead.
As I reach for Your anchor knowing it always holds,
Then I hear Your voice I'm trying to mold.
When I'm in the middle of this raging sea,
Why do I fight to hold onto me?
As the waves come upon me and take me down,
Forgive me Lord, for wearing a frown.

As I surrender in the midst of each wave,
I see more clearly the road that has been paved.
As I stop and seek Your face in each storm,
I become clay in Your hands as You reform.
As I allow You to calm the seas within me,
My spirit rejoices I'm finally FREE.
As I praise Your name for the battle that's won,
Find strength once again and thank God for His Son!

Chapter Eight

The Sinking Vessel

MAY DAY, MAY DAY, can anyone hear me? May Day, May Day, please help me, someone I am drowning. As I continue to sink deeper and deeper in such fear, I cried out to my Heavenly father and asked Him to forgive me of any sin in the name of Jesus. As I asked my Father where are you, I don't want to die, please help me, then I heard Him say (Heb. 13:5) I will never leave you nor forsake you my daughter. Just like Peter as he started to sink after walking on water because he took his eyes off of me and was looking at the wind that was boisterous (Matthew 14:27-33). I was doing the same things in my life.

When Peter reached out his hand for the Lord to take it and then he realized he was safe and how foolish he felt when the Lord said "O you of little faith, why did you doubt (Matthew 14:31)?" I felt as Peter did when he stretched out his hand for the Lord to help me. There will be several times throughout this chapter that I have felt like I was sinking with no one to help me. Usually when I am in the storm and the waves are rough, I can usually overcome that battle through faith and the power of the Holy Spirit. But there was a storm brewing in my life that kept taking me under deeper and deeper for over four years.

Before I reveal what it was in my life that was making me sink, let me tell you about my life. It has been four years that I have dealt with chronic pain. To those ones suffering with chronic pain, pay attention to what I have to say. I allowed the pain to consume my very being. It took over my mind and physical body.

I spent seven days in bed week in and week out. I gave up my independence to who I was and how I felt, an unworthy nobody. My love for God has not changed but the fire in my heart became complacent. As I was praying for a revival for our land, it was my heart that needed revived. Pain, along with any kind of pain pills can cause such an emotional roller coaster in anyone's life.

As I kept going to doctors to help get relief from my pain, I thought I had finally got an answer. My first back fusion was March of 2007 and I never expected the pain to be that bad. The last thing my surgeon said to me was, "expect the pain to be ten times worse then what you can imagine." At the time, my husband and I were staying with my daughter and son-in-law. We were having a house built and that kept me going.

But at night when the pain was so bad I thought about suicide multiple times. I would pick up the bottle of pain pills and would stand and say, I wonder how many it would take. All I wanted at that moment was to close my eyes, sleep forever, and to never feel pain again. Yet, I knew in my Spirit that I loved God too much. I was able to get through the endless days and nights by speaking His word and by singing His songs of deliverance (Psalm 32:7).

What was wrong with me? How could I think about doing such a horrible act? I told God that I love Him too much and my family. How could I do such a selfish act? My daughter took care of me, as my husband and I were getting ready to move into our new house. We were supposed to move in that May but it never happened. A month before as I was in prayer seeking God's face, I told Him if He did not want us in the house to stop it. But how can I pray this when we were getting ready to move in?

I had picked out all the amenities that we wanted, from the color of paint to ceiling fixtures, carpeting, ext., this was my dream house. After living in an apartment for four years I was ready to start my life over. All of a sudden I heard the Lord say **"Walk away"**. I couldn't believe it. I stood there and cried. I called my husband at work and told him what God had spoken to me.

We were both very upset and we didn't know what to do or where to go. The only answer was to obey the Lord and stay in His will or disobey and suffer the consequences. I feared God and loved Him too much not to obey what He spoke to me. We went the following Saturday to tell our real-estate agent that we did not want the house. We asked if we could be refunded the money that we had put towards the house. We had only $500.00 returned to us. I was so devastated that I became deeply depressed.

I told my husband to call this one apartment complex and see if they have any openings for May on the first floor. I had lost all hope of having a home of my own in the midst of everything. Yet, when we found out that my daughter was pregnant after waiting eight long years, we were so overwhelmed with the miracle our God had done. My husband, daughter, and son-in-law had to move us in because I was too sick to help. I moved in once my daughter had the whole place decorated with pictures on the walls and drapes up.

She was almost four months pregnant going on God's strength which enabled her to help me. After we moved in it felt totally different being by ourselves but I had noticed that the pain was getting worse in my back. As I kept going back and forth to my pain management clinic, they kept doing multiple kinds of procedures to help me, but nothing worked. When I found myself getting a morphine pain pump sewed into my stomach, I had a hard time dealing with the pump making my stomach bigger. The months were going by and I found myself in bed more and more.

It was to the place that I could barely function. Then, after three in a half years of living in an apartment, I heard God once again say "you will sell everything you own and move in permanently with your daughter". I said, "Lord, I have all new furniture, it was everything I wanted in my home". He said, "I know, now walk again and sell everything for whatever you can". My daughter and son-in-law just got a four-bedroom house a few months before and I did not want to move in with them.

They needed their time together and to get adjusted to their beautiful baby girl, Hannah. She was definitely a miracle from Heaven and she is the love of my life. My daughter and son-in-law had no objection with us moving in, they knew my health was slowly fading and I was sinking deeper and deeper into depression. The pain was not only in my back, but also down into both of my legs. I could not sit for a long period of time and could not walk without someone helping me, I felt like an unworthy nobody.

I was unable to help my daughter with her new baby or be the wife to my husband that he needed. I was so tired of needles and tests after now having had seven operations on my back. I had a spinal stimulator put in but after almost two years I had it removed. Day in and day out I was sinking deeper and deeper into depression until it finally started to affect my health. I had been admitted into the hospital because I was constantly throwing up.

I will never forget the day when a doctor came into my room. After he examined me, he stood at the bottom of my bed and said to me, "you know what is wrong", but I kept telling him I didn't know. My pastor, my husband, and best friend were in the room with me while the doctor was examining me. The doctor kept saying was "you know what the problem is". As I started to cry, my doctor said, "Roxanne, say the word".

I finally said, "I am not *depressed*". There was the word that he was fighting so hard to get me to say. I felt so embarrassed and ashamed. I thought to myself, a Godly Christian woman cannot be depressed, can she? I silently cried out to God, how could this happen to me, depression is a sin and what is everyone going to think. As I laid in bed I silently said to myself, "who is he talking to, it's surly not me".

As I heard him say about the medication he was going to put me on, I was paying him no attention. I felt so humiliated all I could do was cry. After the doctor left, my pastor said to me, Rox, it is okay. There are a lot of people in this world that are depressed. I told him I know all this but I am supposed to be Godly, I'm supposed to be different.

I had the mindset that because I was Godly, I could not be depressed. Man, was I in denial and being deceived by my own self. It had been over three years since my back fusion and I was getting the same pain back in my legs and lower back. The doctor's answer was to keep increasing my morphine pump but I kept telling them no. I was feeling tired enough without any more drugs going into me.

All I would do was stay in bed every day because the pain was unbearable. I decided to have one more treatment done on my back even though I knew the end results. So why have it? I was a desperate woman looking for just a little relief so I could try to live again. At this point, I had lost all hope and all independence. I had a procedure done on my lower back called microwaving.

The doctor goes in and burns the nerves in you lower back. As I lay there, all I could do was cry from the pain while smelling the nerves being burned. It would take up to six weeks to see if it worked. The first three weeks I had some relief from the pain but the sixth week the pain was unbearable. All I thought about was overdosing on pain pills and killing myself.

I had no hope left and my only option was to have another operation that involved a double fusion. My pain management doctor was totally against it and I didn't know what to do. My choices were to kill myself or go see my back surgeon about the operation. Knowing that I could not kill myself because I loved God too much and second, I could not be that selfish to put my loved ones through that. It has now been over a year since my husband and I have been living with my daughter, son-in-law, and granddaughter.

All I heard over the past year was to wait. I prayed and sought God's face, His word tells us that when we don't know what to do we are to wait on Him (Job 14:14). After a year of waiting, I had to make a decision; I had already lost my independence and who I was. I felt like a worthless crippled with no hope of ever coming out of the cave that I had put myself into (Elijah 19:9). After seeing my orthopedic surgeon he said I would need a double fusion. I stood there and cried. I asked him if I could only get a one level fusion instead of two.

He agreed but not happily and all I could do was thank our God for His favor (Psalm 5:12). My whole family was against this operation, however, I had a peace inside of me that only my God was able to give me (John 14:27). It was May when I saw my surgeon but since we were going on vacation the first week of June, I was scheduled for surgery the third week of June. I ended up flying to Orlando since I was not able to make the long drive. As I was being pushed to my gate, this gentleman came up and starting pushing me.

He kept looking at me; I knew that our Lord had sent him. He looked me in the eyes and said to me "you know Yushua" he said, do not be afraid. All he kept saying to me was how much Yushua loved me and he knows how much you love Him. Yushua want you to know that you will walk upright again. As he leaned over he whispered in my ear and said, "remember you will walk upright again", then he left me sitting there.

I told this man nothing about my upcoming back operation; I know it was all from God. I believe with all my heart that God had sent an Angel to speak those words of encouragement to me (John 12:29). I was so full of hope after that experience. We stayed a week in Florida and returned home. It had been very hard on me and I was so full of pain yet I hid how I felt because I did not want to ruin my family's vacation.

I was anxiously awaiting my surgery and before you know it, the day was here. As my daughter took me to the hospital, I was so nervous and while they were prepping me for surgery my surgeon came in smiling and gave me the news, they had to cancel my surgery. He decided it would be more beneficial to do a two level fusion and since he was leaving town for the weekend it would have to be postponed. I was all ready to go back to the operating room when I got this devastating news. I was so upset; there were no words for me to speak at that time (Ecc. 3:1,7).

As I got dressed and went home, the doctor's office called and said I would have to wait another three agonizing weeks for my surgery. I cried out loud "are you kidding me", I was so full of pain that I didn't care what happened to me. As this vessel was sinking deeper and deeper, all I wanted to do was to be alone. I had finally hit rock bottom and wanted no one around me to witness it. All I wanted was my self pity and my cave (Elijah 19:9).

I did not eat and I could not go to church because I felt so ashamed of myself. I never cared about what people thought of me, but this time of my life I did. As I cried out day and night, *May Day, May Day*, the more I sank. There was a raging sea (Psalm 89:9) going on inside of me and as I cried out to God for His help and fell on my knees, I saw a ray of light. I felt my Lord as He grabbed my hand and pulled me out of the mire and clay (Psalm 40:2).

All of a sudden I heard the voice say to me "why"? I fell on my knees and asked God to forgive me. I was so disappointed that I didn't care. Then I heard my Lord say "you can push through these foxes and keep going believing that all this is for your good (Romans 8:28) or you can choose to stay in your man made cave and lose the race you began (2 Tim 4:7) the day that you opened your heart to me, the choice is yours". At that moment in my life I knew I had to do something. I am going to finish this race in spite of my stinking flesh and me.

I called my pastor and told him what had happened and he told me some things that I needed to change in me. I thank my Heavenly Father everyday for the Godly pastor that He gave me. He is always full of encouragement to me in spite of his own physical pain that he lives with on a daily basis. He is a shepherd who cares very deeply for his flock (Ezekiel 34) and I love him dearly. I told myself that this is a new day with new beginnings.

I determined in my heart that I was going to win this battle come Hell or high waters. I can do all things through Christ that strengthens me (Phil 4:13), I thought. As I wait for the day of my surgery, it was finally here. I was so anxious that I had to get something to calm me down. As my doctor came in and talked to my family and told them the pros and cons, I was already falling asleep from the shot they gave me.

While I was being pushed to the OR room, I couldn't stop crying. I looked around and saw all the tools; I heard them say start counting back word from ten. The surgery took almost five hours, my discs in my back were worse than they anticipated. When I woke up, the pain was unbearable. After five days I was able to go home but it was only the beginning.

I had a nurse and physical therapist come to the house three times a week for almost two months. I can't thank God enough for the daughter He gave me. She took such care of me as she unselfishly gave of herself every day. After about three months, the pain in my back became bearable but why was I sinking deeper and deeper into depression? I fell back into that same old same old trap where I just wanted to be by myself.

I found myself missing church more and more while I alienated myself from my loved ones. Even though my pastor kept telling me I had to push through this, I didn't want to. All I wanted to do was sleep the days and nights away. I blamed it on all the medicine, but the real reason was myself. I felt like such a failure with God, my pastor, and my family.

No matter what anyone said to me, nothing mattered but my bed and I. As the months went by, the pain came back and this time it was affecting my legs. I had to walk with a cane and was falling all the time. When I would go anywhere, I had to always hold onto someone. I wasn't even able to lift my legs so I could cross them.

All I said was what could be next? Every time I think I am coming up to the surface of the water, I find myself going under again. All I could do was to cry out to God, I felt like God had left me (Hebrews 13:5). I knew that if I didn't start to push through the pain and depression and tell Satan to get thee behind me (Matt 16:23) I would only continue to be defeated. I made my mind up that I am a warrior in God's army and come Hell or high water I was going to overcome this battle in my life.

I went back to see my back surgeon to tell him about the pain in my neck, legs, and back again, of course he ordered more tests on me. At that moment I realized that I was like the woman in the Bible who spent all her money on doctors and yet her physical condition remained unchanged (Luke 8:43-48). Like my husband's favorite saying goes, "it is what it is" and my God is able to heal me if that is His will (Matt 26:39). If He chooses not to then His grace is sufficient for me (2 Cor. 12:9). He is the same God who healed me over twelve years ago of kidney and liver failure and He is the same today (Hebrews 13:8).

All I have to do is to believe (John 11:40). I always thought that I was pretty strong in the Lord, but I was so deceived (Matt 24:24). It took me almost four years to realize the deception in my own heart and to repent of it (Job 42:6). Now let me reveal what it was in my life that I couldn't even see. I had allowed fear to consume me each and every day to the point that it paralyzed me.

I allowed doubt to come into my life, while knowing that God had healed me once. In spite of all of the pain I endure daily, its okay. Lord, let the waters rise if you want them to, for I will follow only you. When there is a raging sea going on inside of me, let it bring me to my knees.

THE LIGHTHOUSE

If you find yourself lost in the dark of night,
Just look ahead for the shining light.
As the waves come in with their white caps,
Just read My word, for it is a map.
It will always show you what you should do,
But in myself I do not have a clue.
When you neglect to read the map,
Your spirit becomes weak and your strength will be zapped.
It will never lead you to go the wrong way,
When you obey it you won't go astray.
Just like a ship when it gets lost,
My word will keep you from being tossed.
When the night is to dark that you can't see,
Just reach for My hand and call out to Me.
When you are afraid and cannot move,
Remember my child; how much I love you.
When surrounded by darkness, do not be dismayed,
Allow the Light within you to give off its rays.
Be still and remember that I have won this fight,
So you will no longer fear the darkness of night.
When you feel lost like you are out at sea,
Just allow My Light to shine through thee.

CHAPTER NINE

The Thief in the Night

WHEN YOU THINK ABOUT what a thief does, it can put a lot of fear into a person. A thief will sometimes disguise himself so he cannot be recognized. He has a motive and a plan to steal your property regardless of what it is. A thief will lurk around and stake out his victims before he attacks.

He is self-centered, self-seeking, and self-righteous person. His only concern is for what he can plunder from his victims and how it will benefit him. He does not think about whom he may hurt, how he has to do it, or the consequences of his actions. His only motive is how much he will gain.

He will do whatever it takes to get what he wants, no matter the cost, even if it means killing someone. Jesus warned us in His word that the *thief comes to steal, kill, and destroy, but He came to earth to give use a life and give it to us more abundantly* (John 10:10). A thief wears many disguises. There are many Christians out there who call themselves followers of Christ, but they are only deceiving themselves.

I call these people job comforters. They are quick to condemn and judge you. They try to hinder your faith and your walk with our Lord Jesus Christ. They try to steal your joy, peace, and love, for not only yourself, but for others also. They are the halleluiah, praise the

Lord talkers trying to disguise who they really are, by their phony, self-righteous actions.

The Devil will use whomever he can to get what he wants. This is why Jesus warns us that *even the most elect can be deceived if possible* (Mt. 24:24). Thieves desire only one thing from us and that is our soul. Once you become born again you are a target for an attack from the thief.

He will scope out his victims and use whoever he has to for the kill. It is time for the churches to take off the mask of pretense and allow the Holy Spirit to reveal whom you really are, and whom you are serving. You are either serving Christ or Satan, there is no in between. Elijah told the Israelites to quit wavering between two opinions. *You cannot serve two masters* (Luke 16:13).

You can either chose to serve the giver of life or the thief of life. You will either spend eternity in Heaven or be damned and separated from God in Hell. It is time that the Church protects God's property, and strives to make Heaven their home. *If we have truly denied our-self and picked up our cross daily* (Mk. 8:34), then this thief would not be stealing from God's people. Jesus told Peter, *that on this rock I would build my Church that the gates of Hell will not prevail* (Matt 16:18). When we truly stand believing in God's word and His truth, then there's no thief on earth who can steal, kill, and destroy that which God has given us, His son. No gate of Hell can prevail against God's people as long as we abide in Him and He abides in us.

We must never forget what our Lord has done for us. He paid a price so that we can become God's property. So why is the thief stealing God's property? We have allowed this thief (Satan) to take away that which God has given us. It is time that we who call ourselves Disciples of Christ, reclaim all that we have allowed the thief to steal.

We need to *take the kingdom by force once again for God* (Matt 11:12). We had a couple from our church that needed a place to stay for a week. God spoke to me one Sunday after church and told me that they would be staying with us. Little did I know that Judas was coming through my front door. After the first night with them I knew in my Spirit what this thief was going to try to do.

All I kept saying was, "Lord, I do this all unto you". As we would fellowship and eat meals together, this imposter wore his mask of disguise. As the Holy Spirit kept revealing the truth to me, I had to keep loving them and serving them, no matter what. They ended up staying for three weeks and the last week was the hardest to get through.

I could have never done it without the power of the Holy Spirit. The Peter in me wanted to take out my sword, but the Jesus in me said to love. When we went to church he knew all the right words to say, but he had one plan, to steal, kill, and destroy. He tried to *steal* the respect that my husband and I have for our pastor.

Then, he tried to *destroy* us by planting seeds of doubt by undermining the true word of God. Last, but not least, he tried to *kill* the unity among the brothers and sisters in our church. Little did he know that *I knew the truth that has set me free* (John 8:32). I would not listen to any parts of a watered down, seeker sensitive gospel, that the word has accepted so easily in today's society.

When you walk close with the Lord and have an intimate relationship with Him, He will show you the *wolves in sheep's clothing* (Matt 7:15). Let's not forget about Judas and how he lurked around waiting for the perfect time to betray Jesus. He had a motive, which was to betray the one whom he had ate with, prayed with, talked with, and walked with for the price of thirty pieces of silver. What he thought was going to be a gain, ended up being his biggest loss, his soul.

Judas was saved and still lost his soul. How many of us can love our enemies and call them friend knowing that they're going to betray you? I am thankful to say that through His Spirit, we were able to love them through it all. When they left my house after three weeks, we saw them one time and I knew they were leaving our church.

The enemy's plan failed and God was given all the glory. It is time for our faith to stop being quenched and let it be empowered by the watering of His Holy Spirit. I would have never endured that trial and won the victory if it wasn't for the Lord. It is time for the thief to stop wrecking marriages and families, and time to let God be the repairer of all that is broken.

Let us not forget that this enemy of our soul (Satan) has seen Heaven. He saw its beauty and because of pride, was thrown out never to enter its gates again. So his plan is to stop all of mankind, especially Christians, from making Heaven their home. It is his desire to get us to stumble and fall. Thank God that we have an advocate for our sins and once we repent of any sin, it is forgotten.

We must remember that Jesus is our only access to Heaven. It's not about works, how much money we give, or how much we say we believe in God. It is all about a personal relationship with the Son of God. He's the one who took our fall, bore our pain, and nailed our sins to the cross so we could live with Him. Only He can deliver us from evil.

Let's not forget that there are many thieves out there trying to lead God's children away from truth. We need to be aware of the Judas of this world. They try to fool those one's around them with their lying, persuasive words and lead many astray. They want to get close with us so they can steal that which God has given us.

In these last days, fear will grip our nation, but we who are in Christ do not need to fear. Jesus tells us that *the son of man will come as a thief in the night* (1 Thess 5:2). For believers, there should be an excitement, for the unbeliever, only a fear. Let us not be caught off guard, but always be prepared by living a holy life. For *He has called us to holy as He is holy* (1 Peter 1:16) and to always be watching.

The Lord is speaking to His Church through His pastors, prophets, and His word. Don't let us be like the people in the days of Noah, but let us always *be watching and sober* (1 Thess. 5:6). Jesus would say to His church, "I love you with an everlasting love. I do not want you to be left behind. I have given you the power through my Holy Spirit to be an over comer". *He who endures to the end shall be saved* (Matt 24:13).

"A CRY FOR HELP"

How awesome is my Lord and King,
I lift my voice unto You and sing.
When the pain is too much for me to bear,
I study Your word and know that you care.
As I pray my God please help me understand,
One day my child I'll lead you into the promise land.
When day and night seems to run together,
Your spirit reminds me, with You I'll live forever.
Only You my Lord know all the reasons,
My heart cries out please end this season.
As I hold out my hand for You to hold,
It's better for me to be hot or cold.
As I lift my eyes unto the hills,
My heart longs for only Your will.
As I cry my Lord, take this pain,
You see my tears as they fall like rain.
As I ask my Lord let my life just end,
You whisper to me My Son did I send.
As I preserve to win this fight,
I'm so helpless Lord without your might.
When I pray to my Father
Please strengthen me.
I'll pray Your name for all eternity.
When I am so weak and can't take no more,
I see the cross and how Your body was tore.
As I cry out to You, I need more grace.
That's when I come to You, my hiding place.

CHAPTER TEN

The Overcomer

JESUS CALLED US ALL to be overcomers, but before we can be the overcomers we must first die. We must die to our ways for His ways and for His will. We must allow Him to strip us of all flesh so we can be victorious in all things and be able to walk in the Spirit.

We must be able to say to Him, burn up the dross and bring forth the gold. We must be able to tell the potter to do what He has to do to bring forth a beautiful vessel. It's like painting old walls, if you don't prime the walls before hand and sand out all the rough places, the spots and blemishes will come through no matter how many coats you apply. This is how it is in many believers' lives today. God is trying to sand and make smooth all the rough spots in our lives, but we don't allow Him to finish the work.

We just keep putting on a new coat of paint, but no matter what, the old will always come out if the proper treatment isn't applied beforehand. God says in His word that *He is coming back for a church without spots and blemishes* (Rev. 5:27). We must allow Him to do the necessary work in our lives so we can be like refiners fire, and live an overcomer's life in this fallen world. You see I know all about covering up blemishes in your life.

I have wrestled the past thirteen years with the fear and pain that was in my heart after my husband's unfaithfulness. I thought I had overcome this area in my life until we made the move to Louisiana. I had allowed my flesh to interfere and put the mistrust back into my marriage. I had some dirty spots that had to be cleaned up.

Yes, I love Jesus, went to church faithfully and God used me, but I had blemishes that had to go. God started to show me by His spirit and as I surrendered to Him, He started to strip off the old layers, one at a time. Jesus applied a new coat to me that was the blood of Jesus. Yes, it was painful and yes, it hurt, but I was determined to be an overcomer in this one area of my life.

We must allow Him to strip each and every one of us of all our flesh so we can become more like Him, and less like us. We need to allow God to show us the blessing in the thorn. I would have never thought that all the pain that I had endured, would become my friend, but it has because I allowed God to strip me. Also, He gave me a new coat of His Holy Spirit that in my weaknesses, it has made me stronger in Him.

God knows that there will be times that we fail Him, but the key to overcome is to repent and let God strip us of all flesh so we can be overcomers in all situations. We as believers should strive in this life to become overcomers if we want to be co-heirs with Christ. Only *he who overcomes, and keeps His works until the end, will be given the power over the nation* (Rev. 2:26). It is the believers who have overcome and have persevered in obedience to the end of their life who have the promise of being co-heirs with Christ.

He will share His sovereignty with messianic partners who have proven their trustworthiness in this life by doing the will of God to the end. The believer who overcomes the world is one who has been obedient to God, rather than following the expectations of this world.

Christ has promised this privilege of ruling and reigning with His kingdom and sharing in His royal splendor. Look at the parable of the minas (Luke 19: 17-19).

The one who was given a mina had earned ten minas so Jesus said to him, "well done good servant because you were faithful in a very little, have authority over ten cities". The second came saying, "Master, your mina has earned five minas", likewise He said to him "you also be over five cities". But, the one whom had one mina hid it because of it, his was taken from him. Which was a result in a loss reward, because he was unfaithful.

Does not His word say that, *if you have not been faithful in the unrighteous mammon, who will commit to your trust the true riches* (Luke 16:11). All believers must remember that unfaithfulness will result in loss of reward (Rev. 3:11). If we as believers endure during the hardships and persecutions and keep the faith, then our Lord will reward us when He comes back (2 Tim. 2:12). We must always guard our heart from deception.

So that we do not lose that which we have worked for, but that we may receive a full reward (2 John 8). Every believer has the potential of receiving a full reward or a complete loss of reward. Our faithfulness to Christ is the determining factor for a person's reward. Jesus tells us that, *on this Rock He will build His church that the gates of Hell will not overcome* (Matt. 16:18).

He would ask all of His Churches today, are you built on the solid Rock? We must remember that only those who believe that Jesus is the Son of God will be an overcomer of the world (1John 5:5). We as believers should strive to be an overcomer, so we can receive all of God's promises to us. We must always be ready for His coming and remember that Christ's return will be with expected suddenness.

This should be an incentive to persevere in faithful service, because through misconduct one can lose a crown that has been previously attained (2 John 8). The crown signifies the royal authority given to the victorious co-heirs of Christ. The judgment seat of Christ will be an occasion of either reward or regret (2 Cor. 5:10). His word says, *that if we endure, we shall reign with Him* (2 Tim. 2:12).

Since we are children of God, we are joint heirs with Christ (Romans 8:17). Let all believers remember, God has promised that the faithful believer will be a pillar in the temple, which implies a prominent place of service in Christ's kingdom. He will also receive a new name with the name of the new city of our God, the New Jerusalem. Also, we will receive the right to eat from the Tree of Life, which is in the midst of the paradise of God.

We, the believers who overcome will not be hurt by the second death, but we will be given hidden manna to eat. Also we will receive a white stone with a new name written on it, which symbolizes the victory over the enemies of God, which will not be separated from a new name. This will identify the obedient believer of his or her distinctive character.

He has also promised to give all overcomers the power to rule over all nations (Rev. 2:26). This should be the exalted destiny to which all believers should aspire. He has also promised us white garments, which symbolizes ones recognition of Godly character and faithful service in his life. Also, he has promised not to blot our names from the Lamb's Book of Life, but to confess one's name before the Father and His Angels.

Our Lord will publicly confess one's name before the saints, angels, and the Father, which displays the Lord's approval of one's character and service (Matt. 10:32-33) (1 Tim. 2:12-13). Last, but not least, we have the promise of sharing Christ's throne with Him. This should be the climax to every believer's life, that the faithful Christian will share the actual throne with Christ. Let us not forget that the victory of Christ led to His present position at the right hand of God in Heaven, while the victory of a believer will lead to the privilege of sharing Christ's own earthly throne.

Jesus overcame by humble obedience, even to the point of death, where He was highly exalted to the right hand of God. Believers today who overcome by humble obedience will sit with Christ on His throne (Rev. 20:4-6). Let be reminded that God's purpose in the church is to rise up co-heirs, who will share Christ's authority in His kingdom. These co-heirs must overcome as Christ did by persevering in the faith, despite all suffering.

For as long as we walk with Jesus and serve Him we will have obstacles in our life, therefore we must learn how to be overcomers. This cannot be accomplished in the flesh, but when you walk in the Spirit we can then *overcome by the blood of the Lamb and the word of our testimony* (Rev. 12:11). Our Lord tells us in His word that, *in this world, you will have tribulations, but be of good cheer for I have overcome the world* (John 16:33). So trials and tribulations is a personal relationship with Jesus Christ. For He gave us His promise that, *he who overcomes till the end shall be saved* (Matt. 10:22).

"THE WINNERS CIRCLE"

You said my child just close your eyes,
I'm coming for You, so say your good byes
I'm sending my angles to carry you home,
It is a place where you will not be alone.
Your voice will no longer be heard in this land,
You finished your race now by faith they must stand.
As those around you will morn and cry,
You came out like gold when you were tried.
Because she allowed me to crush and mold,
She sees her loved ones dancing on streets of gold.
She will no longer cry or feel any pain,
She's overcome so the prize she will gain.
She will say to you, just stay on the path,
Then you won't suffer because of God's wrath.
When she stands before the pearly gates,
She bows her head and awaits her fate.
With a loud cry He proclaims enter in,
You entered this race so you can win.
As she stand speechless and struck with awe,
She could not believe all the things that she saw.
As she listens to stories from Saints of old,
She looks around for the one whose heart she does hold.
Where she hears Him say look behind thee,
At that moment she falls and bows her knees.
When He speaks to her a job well done,
She just smiles at Him, her beloved one.

FROM THE AUTHOR

TO ALL THE CHURCHES throughout this land, and to all the souls that read this book: My prayer is that you will see yourself in one of these Churches and know that in your present condition, you need a Savior. The Lord would let you know that no matter what Church you are in or what your present condition is; there is deliverance, healing, and forgiveness in the blood. It doesn't matter what you have done, "for I love you", says the Lord.

"Know that today is the day of salvation. It is not about a religion, it is about a relationship with me. It is not about works, but it is about faith, it's not about living, but about dying to one's self. It's about my will and not the will of man. My arms are open wide and my Spirit is waiting to show you the true condition of your heart.

Come with a repentant heart and I will make all things new", says the Lord. For blessed is the pure in heart, for they see God. To all the faithful followers, keep up the good work and always be strong *to press on towards the mark of the prize which is the high calling of God in Christ Jesus* (Phil. 3:12).

"A WARRIOR'S CRY"

Oh my Father, my God, and my Lord,
How I hunger always for more of Your word.
As I seek Your face on what to do,
You whisper, my child, I'll speak to you.
Just seek my face each waking hour,
Trust in me to give you you're hearts desire.
As I am surrounded by a world of sin,
With your help Lord, this race will I win.
As I see this world spinning round and round,
I cry out to You for Your people are bound.
You said my child they have rejected me,
My people no longer will bow their knee.
As I cry out to You for the people whose lost,
It's all because they no longer want to pay the cost.
As I pray dear Lord just set them free,
You said my people no longer seek after Me.
When I stand in the gap to plead their case,
You speak to my heart; just finish your race.
When I hear you say just lay them down,
And one day very soon, I will give you a crown.

PRAYER

Dear Lord,

I come before you to ask you to forgive me of all my sins. I need you to do the necessary heart transplant surgery to give me a pure heart. Remove all flesh from me and transfer your Spirit into my heart. I surrender my hopes, my dreams, my ways, my life, and my will to follow and serve you, no matter what the cost. Come and wash me by the blood of the Lamb and make me white as snow.

I want you to come into my heart and help me be an overcomer through the power of your Holy Spirit. I acknowledge my need for a Savior and I surrender all. As of this day, I give you my heart and life. Take it Lord, for I am yours through all eternity.

BIOGRAPHY

I HAVE BEEN MARRIED to a loving, caring man for over thirty-seven years. I went on two missionary trips to Israel back in 1994. One was in March and the second in October of the same year. I have been blessed with two sons, one daughter, and seven beautiful grandchildren. I was born and raised in Pennsylvania where I attended an Assembly of God Church for almost ten years and where I had two very successful businesses. The Lord called my husband and myself to Baton Rouge, La. in 2003 with a new job for my husband. We left our house and children (Luke 18:29) and obeyed His calling. After living here for a year, the Lord moved my daughter and son-in-law down here. I attend a Full Gospel Church where the uncompromised word is taught. I am a leader in our women's group were I teach the word. My heart's cry is to do the will of my Father no matter what (Luke 22:42), and to know and obey Him more.

REFERENCE

NOTES

NOTES

NOTES

NOTES

NOTES

NOTES

NOTES

NOTES

NOTES

NOTES

CPSIA information can be obtained at www.ICGtesting.com
Printed in the USA
LVOW07*0007160916

504835LV00005B/11/P